THREAT ASSESSMENTS

For Close Protection & Security Management

Orlando Wilson

Orlando Wilson

Copyright © 2019 Orlando Wilson

Threat Assessments Copyright © 2017 by Orlando "Andy" Wilson. All Rights Reserved.

All rights reserved. No part of this book may be reproduced in any form or by any electronic or mechanical means including information storage and retrieval systems, without permission in writing from the author. The only exception is by a reviewer, who may quote short excerpts in a review.

Cover designed by Orlando "Andy" Wilson

Orlando "Andy" Wilson
Visit my website at www.tohff.com

Printed in the United States of America

First Printing: April 2019

CONTENTS

Title Page
Copyright
THREAT ASSESSMENTS (TA)   1
SECRECY   7
INDIVIDUAL THREAT PROFILE   11
BUILDING SECURITY ASSESSMENT   20
DETAILED BUILDING SURVEY   23
THREAT ASSESSMENT FOR A YACHT TRAVELING TO TURKEY   31
CORPORATE THREAT ASSESSMENT IN DOMINICAN REPUBLIC   42
THE CLOSE PROTECTION ORDERS PROCEDURE   52
EXAMPLE OF INDUSTRIAL SECURITY SITE ORDERS   59
ORLANDO "ANDY" WILSON   68
OTHER BOOKS BY ORLANDO   70

THREAT ASSESSMENTS (TA)

The Threat Assessment (TA) is the most important of all the procedures carried out in any security or business operation but even the most basic TA's are regularly overlooked. The reason for a TA is to identify anything that might threaten you, your team and your overall operation. People carry out basic forms of TA's all the time: Such as, which bars are safe to drink in, where is it safe to walk at night, do I need locks on the windows of my home etc.

A threat assessment must identify all threats that you are exposed to, be it physical assault, injury, terrorism, blackmail, being embarrassed or discredited, health problems, loss of assets or dangerous weather conditions etc. When you identify a threat, you must take procedures to minimize it. In the world of security operations, most people only look for the threat of physical assault, but you must look as deeply as you can and cover every angle.

Consider this, a security company is looking after a client who is being threatened by a potentially violent ex-business partner. The client is married with children. The children have several pets: a cat and a dog. The client lives in a two-story house surrounded by a garden. The security company has identified the threat and decided to install CCTV and provide the client with a team of armed bodyguards. The ex-business partner decides to strike at the client. One night he throws bits of poisoned meat over the wall into the client's garden, which the client's pets eat. When the client and his family wake up in the morning, the pets are dead, and his children are very upset. 1-0 for the opposition. Could this have been avoided, maybe, maybe not. I doubt that many people would consider that a client's family pets would need to be considered in a TA. As I am sure you will agree, such an attack as I have described would be a psychological assault on the client and by upsetting his family especially his children would most probably have more of a profound effect than just physically assaulting him.

When first compiling a TA, you need to get as much information as possible, past, present and future on the person or organization on whom you will be compiling the assessment. Most people may not want to include certain things like extramarital affairs, drug or drinking habits or similar activities. However, it is vitally important that these are included, as they are a source of many potential problems. It would also make sense in a lot of business operations to compile information and profile staff and their family members as they can have access to sensitive information or exert influence over decision makers.

When you compile the threat assessment and a threat is identified, you must find out as much about it as is possible, whether it is an illness or organized criminals. You will need to locate sources of information for your research including social media, news reports, libraries, trade catalogues, directories, public records and the Internet. You need to assess what actions have been taken by a potential threat: verbal abuse, physical assault, theft, tapping your phones or previous medical conditions such as heart attacks, and then you need to know how to counter them.

How you respond to any threats identified will depend on where you are in the world, the local laws, your budget and resources. When a threat is identified research it, and confirm it is realistically a potential problem, and not just a baseless theory from an unexperienced or unreliable source.

In the following chapters are some examples of actual threat assessments that Risks Inc. has compiled over the years. When you read through them you can see some of the topics that need to be included. I have been asked many times by students for templates for threat assessment and my response is always, "MAKE YOUR OWN"!

Every situation is different, as is every client, and in my world, if you are a security professional you should be able to write your own assessments, profiles and reports without having to download generic templates.

The information in this book is a guide, that you can adapt to your own situations and circumstances.

Emergency & Crisis Planning

Professional emergency and crisis planning is what prevents potential problems from turning into disasters. All emergency and crisis planning needs to be kept simple and relevant to the problems they are trying to prevent or minimize. All procedures need to be rehearsed so everyone is clear on what they need to do in an emergency, talking about it is not enough. Plans discussed in comfortable meeting rooms will be enacted in a completely different manner when people are under stress, frightened and things around them are going wrong.

One thing to remember when drawing up your emergency and crisis plans is the simple truth that in reality everything will most likely go wrong. Therefore, you must try to keep your plans as simple and flexible as possible; your plans must be able to adapt to very fluid situations.

Over the years I have come across quite a few "experts" who have drawn up crisis plans for large business and government facilities that were completely unrealistic. One national organization, which had a contract with a local authority, contacted us to put together a 4-hour program designed to train unarmed county security personnel and bus drivers in anti-terrorist and hostage rescue techniques. It took numerous conversations for them to understand it takes more than 4 hours to train a SWAT team and it helps if the students have a little bit of experience. Teaching such techniques to untrained, unfit and inexperienced people simply increases the chances that if there was ever a hostage incident, they would do nothing more than escalate the situation and cause unnecessary casualties. These things are best left to the professionals.

Here are some basic considerations for putting an emergency or crisis management team and plan together for your business or facility.

Team Formation

If you need to put together a crisis team, everyone should know their responsibilities within the team and emphasis any special skills they can offer to the group.

Possible responsibilities of team members could include:

- Team commander
- Sub-commanders
- Dealing with medical emergencies
- Dealing with legal issues
- Media relations
- Security and conflict resolution
- Liaison with outside agencies
- Evacuation and lock down coordination
- Transport and vehicle marshalling
- Search and rescue
- After incident therapy

The Threat Assessment

You will need to compile a threat assessment and identify any potential threats that you or your organization may be under. You will also need to consider what assets and personnel you have available to deal with the threats.

Threats could include:

- Traffic problems
- Drug use or dealing
- Workplace or domestic violence
- Suicides or suicide attempts
- Indecent behavior/sexual predators
- Fire or flooding
- Natural disasters (tornados/hurricanes/earthquakes)
- Theft or loss of assets
- Intruders
- Explosive devices
- Terrorist attacks
- Kidnapping/hostage situations
- Chemical incidents

Basic things you need to consider when dealing with an incident:

- **Communications and incident reporting:** How is the alarm going to be raised and who is going to report to whom?

- **Alerting relevant parties:** How are the relevant personnel for that incident going to be alerted?

- **Incident reaction:** How are you going to deal with that incident?

There is no way I can tell you how to react to every incident, but, based upon my experience, you can expect each one to be different. I'll try to give you some guidelines to make you think, so you can develop your own strategies that are relevant to your own situations.

Here are some considerations if you are putting together emergency plans for a residence or office building. If there is a situation such as an improvised explosive device being found close to your location, you will have two basic choices: You can either stay in the building or evacuate. What you do will depend on the size and location of the device and what your building is made of.

If you choose to evacuate, you should consider:

- How will everybody be alerted to the incident?
- What are the staff responsibilities at all levels, and do those assigned responsibilities know what they are doing?
- Does everyone know the evacuation procedures for their area of the building and what exits will be used?
- Does everyone know where to go after evacuating the building?
- How will everyone be accounted for?
- Will transport be needed to get staff away from the building to a safe area?
- What first aid and emergency help will be available?
- How will people disperse after the incident?

If you choose to stay in the building, you should consider:

- How will the order for a lock down be issued to everyone?
- What are the staff responsibilities at all levels?
- Do those who are assigned responsibility know what they are doing?
- Does everyone know where the safe areas are within the building?
- How will people be alerted that the incident is over or that they need to evacuate the building?

The above is just a guide to get you thinking, emergency and crisis planning is a very detailed job. There is more to it than printing a form from the internet and just ticking a few boxes!

SECRECY

Nothing is as important as secrecy. All your security plans and preparations will be worthless if the bad guys know them. Good personal and operational security begins with a clear understanding of what kind of information the criminals will be trying to learn about you, your family or business operation.

Governments must keep secret their diplomatic alliances, secret treaties and military strategies etc. Although a government may suffer a great loss because of poor security, it is hard to imagine today a situation where a nation's defenses could be completely overwhelmed by a single security leak, not so with a small-scale operation. A company might be ruined as the result of a single security leak. A family might be ambushed and kidnapped because a single piece of information was found out by the criminals, such as a home address, security procedures, or the routes your child takes to school or their travel itinerary.

Things that should be kept secret and restricted:

• Addresses and identities of individual employees, their families, or close friends.

• Security plans and methods of operation.

• Transportation capabilities.

• Sources of supplies.

• Available back up.

• The location of hideouts and safe houses, etc.

• Codes, signals, passwords, and lines of communications.

Good personal security is a must, good team security begins with good personal security. If a person is living or traveling under their own name, they must keep information about their occupation and activities limited to those who need to know only. There is no one more completely defenseless than the individual whose personal security has been compromised.

Personal security is a 24/7 job, to some it comes almost instinctively but others can find it very hard to develop. An individual's habits and personality will have a considerable effect on their attitude towards personal security; some people will just never get it and can be a liability. Such people should not be allowed access to sensitive information or taken to high-risk locations.

The Basic Principals Of Security

• **Deception:** Deception is essential to the success of all security operations, always have a cover story and be ready with feasible explanations as to who you are, what you're doing and why you are doing it.

• **Avoiding attention:** One way for any individual or organization to seriously compromise their security is to attract attention. Always keep a low profile and remember that if people don't know what you are doing, they cannot counteract you.

• **Self-Discipline:** Everyone must abide by the rules, if anyone disregards the security program, they could jeopardize the personal security of all involved.

• **The program:** A security program must be outlined and made clear to all personnel. Everyone must be trained and willing to work within the program.

• **Continual inspection:** The biggest thieves are usually those trusted with the largest responsibilities - they have access to assets or information worth stealing. The conscientious person with the flawless record can easily deviate by their own accord or under the pressure of a little blackmail. People change and so does the importance they place on their own security, given time people will relax. This is why there is a need for everyone to be constantly inspected.

- **Fluid change:** This is best illustrated by frequent changes of meeting places, routes and operational procedures to keep the criminals guessing. This principle is necessary because, if given enough time, professional criminals can crack the security of any organization. So, old security measures must be constantly and fluidly replaced and updated.

- **Action:** If someone is not capable of obeying the security program they will need to be disciplined, they should not be trusted or only trusted with information or tasks that will not jeopardize anyone else.

You will not have a security program by following only one or more of these principles, all must be followed, and you must remain alert 24/7.

Basic Counter-Intelligence

Basic counter-intelligence increases the security of all operations and the chances of surprise in offensive operations. Your security program, even if it is for yourself, should be developed to prevent information leaks, or situations where criminals can extract information from you or your business. You must initially try finding criminal sympathizers already within your operation; this could be your locally recruited secretary or attorney. If you detect a sympathizer within your operation, what are you going to do, fire them or feed them false information? You should also consider why they sympathize with the criminals, is it for money or are they being threatened. Counter-intelligence can be broken down in the two practices, denial and detection.

Basic denial operations may include:

- Thoroughly brief everyone on how the criminals will try to get information on you, your personnel, and your operation.

- Place a high emphasis on the security of information. People must understand to keep things on a need-to-know basis and not to talk about confidential subjects in public.
- Make sure all papers, old computers and communication devices etc. are properly disposed of.
- Employees should be briefed on bars, clubs and other venues that are safe to frequent and those that are not.

Basic detection operations may include:

- Background investigations must be done on all employees, especially locals who have access to confidential information.
- Make maximum use of CCTV, covert cameras for detection and overt cameras for deterrence.
- Monitor your staff communications including e-mail and telephone calls.
- Put any staff members acting suspiciously or who seem to be living beyond their means under investigation and surveillance.

These are just some basic considerations, but they can make your security program into something that would make it extremely difficult for the bad guys to gain information on you. If they cannot get any information on you, it makes their job of targeting you a lot harder. Hopefully, so hard they'll go and do what we want them to do, find and easier target of which there are plenty.

INDIVIDUAL THREAT PROFILE

Here is an example of an individual threat profile that can be used to build up information on the person you are compiling the TA on, this could be yourself or a known criminal.

If the information compiled is used properly it can help you to predict a criminal's potential plan of action and aid law enforcement agencies in apprehending them. If the threat profile is compiled on a potential client, it can highlight not only any threats they could be under but also if they would be a credible client and able to do such things as pay their bills on time.

I always tell my students to check out their clients and ensure they know who they are and why they are looking for security or investigation services. I have had several incidents where clients were not truthful regarding their need for investigations services. One client was an American Investigations company that I believe knew of the criminal issues with the case they asked us to work on in Russia but did not let us know because the price would have gone up. Luckily, we were using a very experience investigator who was able to deal with the issues he encountered, luckily… Trust is just a word that has no place when dealing with new clients, it's business, its money, so always cover your ass and take nothing at face value!

Not everything in the following checklist will apply to everyone and this is only a guide of the type of information that can be of use. Most of the below should be self-explanatory but I have added some notes to explain why a few of the topics can be important.

Individual Threat Profile

ORLANDO "ANDY" WILSON

Date / /   File Number: Compiled by:

1. Surname:

2. First names:

3. Alias:

4. Title: Mr./Ms./Mrs.

5. Date of birth:

6. Height:

7. Weight:

8. Build:

9. Complexion:

10. Eye color:

11. Hair color:

12. Handicaps:

13. Scars and tattoos:

14. Fingerprints taken:

15. Ethnic background:

16. Nationality and passport number:

17. Photographs:

18. Preferred jewelry & clothing: For identification

19. Occupation:

20. Earnings: Can they afford your services or have the fund to hire a hitman

21. Marital status:

22. Home address:

23. Type of residence:

24. Who else lives there: Problems from neighbors of house guests...

25. Home phone number:

26. Personal e-mail:

27. Mobile phone number:

28. Description of vehicles used:

29. Business addresses:

30. Business phone numbers:

31. Business fax numbers:

32. Business e-mail:

33. Other addresses:

34. Other phone numbers:

35. Other fax numbers:

36. Social networking sites used: Are they secure and what are they showing.

37. Names used on social media: Ensure you know all sites and names.

38. State of health:

39. Medication needed:

40. Recreational user of illegal or prescription drugs: Ask around if required!

41. Doctors name and contact details:

42. Duress and stress signals: Important if they have a temper or heart condition!

43. Places frequented both professionally and privately:

44. Languages spoken:

45. Lawyer's contact details: For if they are arrested or need enlightening.

46. Financial status: Do they actually have money?

47. Any bad debts, if yes to whom:

48. Banks used:

49. Religion:

50. Religiously active: Can affect diets or attract threats.

51. Criminal record:

52. Known current criminal activities and affiliations: Criminal friends?

53. Known to law enforcement agencies:

54. Mode of operation:

55. Known personal and business associates:

56. Known opponents/enemies:

57. Future goals:

58. Sexual orientation in public and private: Potential for blackmailed

59. Political & freemason affiliations:

60. Eccentricities & habitual behavior:

61. Details of spouse or partner:

62. Details of children and other family members:

63. Details of other direct family, including aliases and maiden names:

64. Extramarital affairs, details of whom with: Major potential for blackmail

Example Of A Threat Profile – Edited

Date: ## /## /####   File Number: #########

Person of Interest
- Name: Tony Fredrick Maple (Age 59yrs)
- Height: 5'6"
- Weight: Approx. 140lbs

- Hair: Dark Brown/Receding
- Eyes: Brown
- Build: Slim
- Married: Unknown
- Email Address: maple99@d#d.cm

Associated Addresses and Registered Phone Numbers:

- ## Hibiscus Court, Miami, FL 33###. Probable primary residence
- Phone Residence: (786)###-####
- Phone Mobile: (561)###-####
- ### Sentry Drive, DelRay Beach, FL 33###. Probable rental property
- Phone Residence: (561)###-####
- Phone Residence: (561)###-####
- Phone Mobile: (727)###-####
- "JoJo's Bar & Grill" ### Stroop Street, Chicago, IL 60###
- Phone Business: (201)###-####
- Web: http://jojochicago/

Confirmed Family:

- Ron Maple
- Relationship: Younger Brother
- Location: Unknown exact location – possibly Germany
- Occupation: Real Estate Developer
- Wife: Jenny Maple: Interior designer
- Children: Sacha Maple, Emily Maple, Robert Maple

Tony Maple Summary

Mr. Maple is a very successful German/American businessman who owns interests in adult entertainment locations in Philadelphia, Chicago and San Francisco and a successful beauty salon business in New Jersey, Chicago and Miami Beach. Mr. Maple also owns four single-family residential properties in South Florida and two multi-family residential properties in New York City.

Mr. Maple maintains a high social profile, mainly through his beauty salon related business, and has a fairly high social network profile through business-related media articles, blogs and websites. There have also been a number of biographical mediums written about Mr. Maple; however, the majority of these pieces eventually turn into business-related articles. Interestingly, a biographical article from ##### dated 22 May, 2016 (http://www.#######.com/1.479931) goes into more detail about Mr. Maple's political leanings, his past dealings with high ranking New York government officials and his relationship with his younger brother, Ron. At the time of the writing of the ##### article, Mr. Maple described his support for abortion and transgender rights which led to serious differences between him and his brother, Ron.

As with most high-profile, successful businesspeople, the risk of reputational damage looms large. A check of open-source databases reveals that Mr. Maple maintains a low-key personal lifestyle. In the past 2 years, Mr. Maple has been involved in two civil litigations: one involving his ex-business partner and one against the City of Miami Commercial Licensing Department. No other involvement with either the civil or criminal legal systems could be located.

After reviewing open-source information on Mr. Maple, the following have been determined to be the greatest potential negative occurrences:

- **Reputational Threats:** This could come about through a number of ways; however, the most likely would arise through perceived "bad" business dealings, hurt feelings stemming from court decisions or from those who disagree with his stated political views. As Mr. Maple seems to maintain high business and social standings, the risk of this occurring remains low; however, would require constant monitoring to ensure that potential threats are mitigated.

• **Social Life:** Mr. Maple states that he is heterosexual but employees at his Miami businesses state that he is Gay/Bi-Sexual, this opens up the potential blackmail threat he is under. In his social circle the use of recreational drugs is common.

• **Personal Physical Threats:** Being a person who is known to many in the general public, and one whose financial gains have been greatly publicized, Mr. Maple must be considered a target by those who would desire to take what he has earned or to simply see him put under physical duress. Threats of this nature could occur thusly:

1. Someone who might recognize Mr. Maple and begin verbally assaulting him.
2. Someone who would want to kidnap Mr. Maple, a family member or associate for the purpose of extorting a ransom.
3. Someone who would want to inflict bodily harm to Mr. Maple, a family member or associate.
4. Someone who would want to kill Mr. Maple, a family member or associate.

Mitigating these threats will include the following steps:

• A thorough personal profile on Mr. Maple; one in which he reveals key information regarding family, social partners, past experiences that could pose current and future problems, etc.

• Security surveys of Mr. Maple's residences which he will occupy.

• Security surveys of business premises where Mr. Maple has offices that he works from.

• Risk assessments of all upcoming travel that is to be undertaken by Mr. Maple. If required, advance teams to conduct risk assessments and security surveys at destination(s).

• Threats to Physical Assets: These are threats to physical assets owned by or associated with Mr. Maple.

1. **Transportation:** All vehicles, vessels and aircraft owned by Mr. Maple will have to be identified and verified. Verification will take place through Mr. Maple providing a list of all items and photographs obtained of each item – including all identification markings (license plates, aircraft and vessels registration numbers). It is recommended that, prior to use, the method of transportation is thoroughly checked and left in a protected area until used.
2. **Structures:** All buildings (residential and commercial) owned by Mr. Maple will have to be identified and verified. Mr. Maple will provide addresses to all buildings he owns. Site visits to each location will be required for the purpose of conducting physical security surveys.
3. **Threats to Family Members:** This Biographical Profile of Mr. Maple has only been able to confirm one relative; his younger brother Ron Maple. A full disclosure by Mr. Maple of all his relatives would be required for the purpose of properly vetting and identifying them.

• Ron Maple's exact location would have to be verified. At this time, it would appear that he and his family reside primarily in Germany; however, he is associated with the following address: ### NW 24th Avenue, Boca Raton, FL, 33###

It should be noted that this address seems to be a rental property, furthering the importance of verifying his and any other family members location.

Miscellaneous Threats:

• **Political Threats:** Mr. Maple has gone on record as being very pro-abortion and for LGBT rights. This political stance may become a potential motivation for threats against Mr. Maple.

• **Religious Threats:** As a high-profile and extremely successful person, Mr. Maple could become the target of anti-LGBT motivated individuals or groups.

• **Internal Medical Threats:** A full-disclosure medical profile would have to be provided by Mr. Maple to determine steps (if any) that would need to be taken by Close Protection personnel to mitigate any existing medical conditions.

• **External Medical Threats:** The number of mosquito-borne infectious diseases continue to grow in Florida. West Nile Virus, Dengue Fever and Zika infected people are becoming more common in the Miami-Dade region. A threat assessment of Mr. Maple's residence should be undertaken to determine the level of threat posed by mosquitos and identify mitigation measures that could be imposed to lower the risk.

All information contained in this document has been retrieved feom open-source networks. To be declared accurate, all information must be verified through interviews with Mr. Maple and physically through security surveys.

BUILDING SECURITY ASSESSMENT

Below is an example of an assessment that was compiled on an apartment complex in Miami Beach after one of the units was broken into several times, and the tenants were considering suing the owner for security negligence.

Date: ##/##/####   File Number: #########

Location: Apt ##, ## ###### Miami Beach, FL, 33###

The front of the building, East Side

The front entrance to the building is completely open with no visible security or deterrents to trespassers. Anyone can walk off the street and up to the apartments.

Possible procedures that could be put in place to deter trespassers include:

• Properly placed lights that illuminate all dark areas. The evening, I viewed the building, there were lights out in one of the stairways; this could also be a safety concern for tenants/guests and a liability concern for the building management.

• Security cameras could be placed to cover the main entrance or dummy security cameras could be placed in obvious locations to act as a deterrent to possible trespassers.

• Signs could be placed in obvious locations stating that the building has security cameras, and trespassers will be prosecuted, etc.

Rear and side perimeters

There did not seem to be any fences or barriers around the building that could stop a possible trespasser. The walls and fences would be easy to climb or cross for the average person.

Possible procedures that could be put in place to deter trespassers include:

• Properly placed lights, possibly on motion detectors can be placed in all dark areas.

• As with the front of the building, cameras and signs can be used to deter possible trespassers.

• The perimeter fencing needs to be replaced with something that will stop trespassers. There is no point having locked gates, if people can just jump a wall or fence a few yards away.

Walkways: There is nothing stopping people walking from the street onto the 1st floor walkways. Lockable gates could possibly be placed at the bottom of the steps leading to the walkways.

Apartments

• The doors of the apartments need to be fitted with good locks and inspected to ensure that the locks cannot be opened through a nearby window. The door frames also need to be inspected to ensure they are solid. All locks on external doors need to be changed after tenants' leases are expired and before new tenants take over the apartment; I believe this is required under Florida law.

• The apartment windows are in no way secure and are easily opened from the outside. These windows need to be replaced.

• The shutters on the inside of the windows could be alarmed and would provide warning for occupants of an intruder gaining access to the apartment. The shutters themselves are flimsy and could not stop anyone trying to gain access to the apartment, but some form of dead bolt could be put in place to deter anyone from using excessive force to gain entry.

• Internal alarms could be used but it must be remembered these only alert others during a break-in, they do not prevent break-ins. If alarms are to be put in place, they must be serviced and tested regularly.

Conclusion

In my professional opinion, the building and the apartments' security level is extremely low. I personally would not be comfortable leaving valuable assets or having close friends, etc., living in the building. The main weakness is the easy accessibility to the apartments from the street and the ease of access to the apartments that can be gained through the windows.

These days with crime rates on the increase the building management and landlords need to understand that they are legally liable for the security and safety of their tenants.

DETAILED BUILDING SURVEY

Here is a template for a detailed building security survey in potentially hostile environments. As you read through you will see that some of the things mentioned will not be applicable if you are assessing the security for a business, house or apartment in areas where there is low level crime and no serious active threats. As I said earlier, use this as a guide and take what is useful for you.

1. Identification

a. Local and Official Name (from map study).

b. General Location and Address.

c. Map References. Identify by map series, sheet number, and edition.

d. Grid references and GPS coordinates

e. Additional Information. Indicate any peculiar information, date of original survey, and any updates if applicable.

2. Surrounding Area

a. General Information.

(1) General overview. Include aerial photograph{s).

(2) Map references.

(3) Additional information.

b. Tactical Considerations.

(1) Command posts (CP's). Include the following information:

(a) Entrance(s) and approach routes.

(b) Security, cover, and concealment.

(c) Provisions for water, electricity, telephone, ventilation, rest rooms, adequate working space, and satellite communications antennas.

(d) Who owns the building, the address, the point of contact (POC), facilities available in the area, and vehicle and foot approach routes to the building. (Ensure the CP is shown on the surrounding area sketch, and if possible, show photographs of the building and area.)

(2) Surveillance/sniper positions. Include the following.

(a) An overwatch of the area.

(b) Concealed access routes to the CP and staging areas.

(c) Secured and concealed accesses and/or entrances to the surveillance position.

(d) Cover and concealment of the surveillance position from observation by personnel located on the location.

(e) Provisions for water, electricity, and restroom facilities.

(f) The location of the surveillance position on the surrounding area sketch. (Show photographs of the building in which the surveillance position is located, the surveillance position in the building, the view from the surveillance position to the location, and the view from the location to the surveillance position.)

(g) A description of the following: 1. Type of building. 2. Number of stories. 3. Location of surveillance position in relation to the location. 4. The area to be used by the observer. 5. Who owns the building, address, POC(s), and their telephone numbers. 6. Access routes to the area.

(3) Staging areas. Include the following:

(a) Whether the structure has a basement or other large area concealed from outside view.

(b) If the staging area is in the vicinity of the location preferably in the surrounding area.

(c) Suitability for holding number of personnel for how many days.

(d) Provisions for water, electricity, and rest rooms available, if possible.

(e) Whether routes to the CP are concealed from observation by personnel located on the location.

(f) Concealment of accesses (for example, underground parking lot}.

(g) The location of the staging area in relationship to the location, who owns the building, POC for access and his telephone number, recommended approaches to the area, and recommended entrances. (Show the location of the staging area on the surrounding area sketch and photographs of the building and the area.)

(4) Recommended approaches. Include the following:

(a) Main direction from the staging area to the location and surveillance positions.

(b) Whether approach is by air, land, or water.

(c) Whether it is by vehicle or foot.

(d) Any unusual circumstances about the approach (for example, an approach over rooftops of surrounding buildings, facilities such as banks located near the approach that may have 24-hour guards).

(e) Blind or insecure spots on the approaches.

(f) If possible, photographs of the route from the staging area to the location along the recommended approach.

(5) Sanctuaries. Include the following information:

(a) Friendly government embassies, churches or residences in the area.

(b) The building and the area to be used as the sanctuary.

(c) Who owns the building, the address, the POC and telephone number(s), location in relation to the location, and what the facility is normally used for.

(d) Location of the sanctuary in relation to helicopter landing zones (LZ's) and evacuation routes.

(e) Location of the structure on the surrounding area sketch. (Show photographs of the building and, if possible, of the area to be used as sanctuary.)

(6) Obstacles and/or danger areas. Include the following information:

(a) Vegetation and terrain surrounding the location.

(b) Open areas (for example, large avenues adjacent to the location).

(c) Locations of guarded banks or other guarded facilities, hostile country embassies, and threat group offices.

(d) High crime areas and the most common type of criminal occurrence in these areas.

(e) Roadways or avenues recommended for approaches that are affected by rush hour traffic.

(f) Checkpoints, curfews, police or security patrols, universities, construction areas, police or military installations.

(g) Exceptionally well illuminated areas around the location.

3. Ground description

(a) General Description. Always orient the direction of the survey to main geographical points. Pay particular attention to basic locations, type of construction, distances from perimeter barriers to principal structures and then structures of a secondary nature to the principal structures.

(b) Perimeter Barrier. Total information coverage is required. Emphasize heights, widths, and thicknesses. Zero in on weak spots and describe them in detail.

(c) Entrances to Grounds. Examine points of normal or prepared access, style of construction, security and/or locking devices, closed-circuit televisions (CCTV's), and guards.

(d) Structures. Include any additional structures located on the grounds.

(e) Terrain and Vegetation. Provide a very simple description (for example, height and type of trees).

(f) Additional Information. Include possible routes of access and masking effect of vegetation.

4. Building description

a. Exterior. Give a general description to include basic style of construction. Refer to aerial photographs, if available.

b. Entrances to Building. Give a detailed description including names of entrances, if applicable.

(1) Main entrances. Working from outside to inside, describe the entrance and any entrance procedures, if applicable. Describe hinges from the top down.

(2) Other entrances. Describe the same as above.

(3) Emergency entrances and exits. Describe the same as above.

(4) Additional information. Include grates, air conditioning ducts, fans, and trap doors,

c. Interior Description of Building.

(1) General description.

(2) Floor plans. Refer to attached floor plans and floor plan sketches.

(3) Floors. Include type of construction of the floors from the basement up.

(4) Corridors. State width, height, type of lighting, type of floor

covering, depths of doorways, and general information.

(5) Stairways. Describe by name if possible and describe the locations of landings and banisters. Give the number of stairs.

(6) Elevators. Include mechanism, escape hatch, and other contents of the elevator (off the data plate) including any limitations of the elevator (for example, that it does not service the top floor).

(7) Doors and locks. Refer to a specific industry or professional standard door/lock/key chart available to all participating organizations.

(8) Windows and locks. Describe standard type(s) for the specific structure and any exceptions.

(9) Physical barriers. Describe any barrier system that will be used during an emergency.

(10) Hardened areas. Describe in detail.

(11) Weak points. Describe in detail.

(12) Additional information. Describe in detail.

d. Roof.

(1) General description. List antennas, elevator rooms, and type of construction.

(2) Entrances and exits. Describe in detail, with emphasis on areas of weak construction.

(3) Fire escapes and ladders. Describe in detail.

5. Common Systems

a. Security.

(1) Personnel.

(a) Security guards. Give the numbers, are they competent and types of weapons carried.

(b) Security detail and/or bodyguard. Describe the same as above.

(c) Contract watchmen. Give the numbers, are they competent,

THREAT ASSESSMENTS

types of weapons, and times of shift changes.

(d) National policemen. Give the numbers, are they competent and affiliation with the facility.

(2) Total security equipment. Include a total inventory of all security equipment.

(3) Sensors and alarms.

(a) Location outside.

(b) Location inside.

(c) Communications.

(d) Organic Transportation.

(e) Medical Equipment.

(f) Power. (1) Explain primary, normal system (for example, source and shutoff data). (2) Explain backup and emergency system(s) (for example, source, shutoff data, and duration capability). (3) Provide additional information. (4) Air Conditioning and Ventilation. Explain the air conditioning system, with special emphasis on vents and air intakes. (5) Sewage and Drainage. Explain the sewage system that services the structure with a special emphasis on access to the structure, if any. (6) Additional Information.

6. Personnel Structure

a. Staffing Pattern.

b. Key Personality Data.

c. Additional Information.

(1) Draw north arrows on the photographs and annotate items of importance on them. Do not annotate on a photograph an item indicated on the legend and/or label, unless necessary.

(2) Assemble finished product in the following order: (a) Table of contents. (b) Narrative description. (c) Surrounding area sketch. (d) Photograph and/or slide index. (e) Photographs with labels,

north arrows and annotations. (f) Slides.

(3) Have another person check for accuracy.

NOTE. Attached as an enclosure should be the door/lock/key reference information. The standard format for the door system should be very simple and not require a great deal of time either to collect information against or to produce a survey from. The survey should be specifically prepared: 1. List all doors. 2. Note whether they are standard or not, giving a definition of what a "standard door" for that particular structure is. 3. Describe any door that is not standard

THREAT ASSESSMENT FOR A YACHT TRAVELING TO TURKEY

Assessments for travel management and security are extremely important as is the briefing of the travelers. Once a travel assessment has been compiled then the travelers need to be briefed on what information and procedures are relevant to them. From a close protection perspective, the clients might not want a full security brief, that's why they hired a security team to take care of them, but if there are specifics that apply to them then the team leader should brief them. There is usually no need for the clients to know all the details of an assessment, unless of course they want to, I always give them the option.

Date: ## /## /2008   File Number: #########

Overview

The Eastern Aegean and Western Turkey areas are considered as the meeting points of Europe and Asia. This area has been important to trade since Biblical times. The Eastern Aegean leads to the Sea of Marmora, that connects to the Black Sea, the route through the Bosphorus Strait and the Dardanelles is now a vital artery for oil coming from Central Asia.

The Eastern Aegean is a politically complicated area due to the disputes between Greece and Turkey over various islands and tracks of sea. The Aegean Sea has about 1,415 islands and islets, of which 1,395 belong to Greece.

Maritime Crime

Although acts of maritime piracy in the Eastern Aegean seem to be extremely rare in modern times, petty crime should be expected to be at the regular level. That said, in January 1996 a passenger ferry was hijacked in the Black Sea by Chechen terrorist for 4 days. Due to the ongoing anti-terrorist operations in the Caucasus, Iraq and Afghanistan, there is a potential threat of high-profile hijackings to publicize the terrorists causes.

Shore Side Crime

Street crime figures are relatively low in Turkey, although it is on the increase in large urban areas. As in other large metropolitan areas throughout the world, common street crimes include pick pocketing, purse snatching, and mugging. Be wary of approaches from strangers offering to change money or offering tea, juice, alcohol, or food, which may be drugged. Two common drugs used are Nembutal and Benzodiazepine which, when used incorrectly, can cause death. In 2007 a high number of sexual assaults on foreigners, including rape, were reported in coastal tourist areas in Southwestern Turkey.

While walking or shopping beware of pickpockets who operate in any crowded place such as on a bus, tram, metro or entrances to busy locations where people are packed close together, guard your bag, wallet, camera, jewelry, wristwatch, and anything else of value. Other street crime methods include bag-slashers who get behind or beside you in a crowded place, slash your bag or pocket with a razor blade and collect your valuables. If they are good and they usually are, you won't see or feel a thing. Bag-snatchers are often young boys, they will grab your bag and run, if your bag is snatched do not to pursue the thief, even young boys in Turkey often carry knives and can be dangerous.

There are many cases of tourists being invited to visit clubs or bars, only to be vastly overcharged for drinks. For example, a couple may go into one of these places and order a drink. When they are presented with the bill, however, they find it to be for a thousand dollars. When they protest, they are confronted by a couple of thugs who show them the price list for drinks, which is well-hidden behind the bar. It is not unusual for a glass of Coke to be 3 to 4 hundred dollars. How things develop will depend on the club and the victims. In most cases the victim will have their wallets emptied and may be escorted to an ATM machine and instructed to draw out more money or just beaten and robbed. If there is more than one victim, one may be held in the venue while the other is sent to get more money.

Public Transport

Caution should be used when using public transport. Trams are a favorite location for pickpockets and bag slashers. Overcharging by taxi drivers, particularly by those in popular tourist areas is common. Pay attention to what denomination of bill you are using to pay for the fare, taxi drivers switching money and claiming you gave a smaller denomination than what you thought is a common scam. Only utilize taxis with meters, sit in the back seat and do not accept food or drink from the driver. Try to ensure the driver sticks to the main roads, if you are uncomfortable with the driver pay them and get out the car when safe to do so.

Driving

When renting motor vehicles outside of EU and US stick to the main international companies such as Hertz etc. The safety standard of rental vehicles may not be the same as EU and US and driving may be more hazardous. In many developing countries, if you are involved in a traffic accident with locals you will be at fault just because you are a foreigner.

Counterfeits

Counterfeit and pirated goods are widely available in Turkey, many of which are produced within the country. Counterfeits can include designer clothes, sunglasses, DVD's, software, perfumes, toothpaste, etc. Buying such products may be illegal under local law, which may not be rigorously enforced until the local authorities just want to make a statement. Bringing counterfeit and pirated goods to the EU and US may result in forfeitures and fines. Using counterfeit deodorants, toothpastes etc. also pose health risks.

There have been two cases in Altinkum within the past few months of counterfeit British 20-pound notes being reported by money changers. In both cases those accused, British citizens, were arrested and imprisoned until their court hearings. It seems strange that these two cases would occur in the same area of Turkey within a short period of time with the accused in both cases being apparently unrelated. Always use established banks to change money, because many small currency exchange agencies are used by organized crime as fronts for money laundering operations.

Police And The Law

The police and judicial system have a reputation for being hard and human rights violations are common. In tourist areas the police will be more accommodating to tourists but not forgiving where crime is concerned. Convictions of foreigners set good examples that the police are doing their job and for tourists to behave. In some areas crimes such as physical and sexual assaults on tourists by locals may not be taken seriously by the local police or the blame laid on the tourist's actions. This is where contacting your local embassies and consulates is important to report such crimes.

Basic Regulations And Laws (Uk Foreign Office)

• There is now a smoking ban on all forms of public transport (trains, ferries and taxis) and in outdoor venues (including stadiums and playgrounds). Transitional arrangements are in place for cafes, bars and restaurants; they too will come under the smoking ban in July 2009. You risk being fined 62 YLT if you are caught smoking in a designated smoke-free area.

• Turkey has strict laws against the use, possession or trafficking of illegal drugs. If you are convicted of any of these offences, you can expect to receive a heavy fine or a prison sentence of 4 to 24 years.

• The export of antiquities is prohibited and carries a prison sentence from five to ten years. The use of recreational metal detectors is against the law.

• Dress modestly if visiting a mosque or a religious shrine.

• It is illegal not to carry some form of photo ID in Turkey. It is therefore advisable to carry a photocopy of your passport with you at all times.

• Do not take photographs near military or official installations. You should seek permission before photographing individuals.

• Homosexuality is not illegal but is not widely tolerated: public displays of affection could result in prosecution for public order offences.

• It is an offence to insult the Turkish nation or the national flag, or to deface or tear up currency.

The Turkish Mafia

Organized crime has long established roots in Turkey and the Turkish Mafia has a brutal reputation and is one of the main players in the heroin business. Turkey is and always been an established trade route between Asia, Middle East and Europe. It is now an establish trafficking crossroads for heroin heading into EU and synthetic drugs heading into Asia. In recent years Turkey has also become a major route for people traffickers moving people into Western Europe from Asia. Once in Turkey the goods to be trafficked, be they people, cigarettes, drugs or counterfeit cosmetic products start or continue their journey west via land or more likely by sea from Turkey's Southern or Western coastline.

Turkey is also a major market in the domestic and international sex trafficking trade. Usually, women from the former Soviet states are brought to Turkey knowingly to work in the sex trade or on false pretenses and enslaved. From Turkey the women are trafficked internationally.

Prostitution is legal under Turkey's legal system. Prostitutes have mandatory weekly health checks and are issued identity cards by the local authorities. They operate out of brothels that are guarded by the local police. Note: There is a large transsexual and transvestite community in Turkey the vast majority of whom work in the sex industry.

Terrorism

Russian peace keeping operations in the Republic of Georgia and the Caucasus. There is little chance of terrorist incidents related to the military actions in the Republic of Georgia. There has been over the years numerous terrorist incidents in Turkey in protest or Russian anti-terrorist operations in Chechnya and Dagestan against Muslim extremists. Both Russia and Georgia are orthodox Christian countries, so the Islamic community has little interest. The separatists in South Ossetia and Abkhazia are controlled by Russia as the Georgians are controlled by the US, any acts of terrorism would be counterproductive for both sides cause and would not be tolerated by Russia or US.

- Turkey, the PKK and Iraq the issues with Turkey and the Kurds of Eastern Turkey date back to after the first world war. The PKK (Kurdish Workers Party) was formed in the 1970's. The PKK are an active terrorist organization and have close links with the Kurdish Peshmerga militia that are the de facto army of northern Iraq. This has led to Turkish forces regularly mounting ground and aerial operations into Northern Iraq to target active terrorist groups who have sanctuary there. The war between Turkey and the Kurdish terrorists has been a low intensity dirty war with an estimated cost of 40,000 lives. This conflict is likely to continue well into the future.

• Terrorist kidnappings. During the early and mid-1990s, the PKK kidnapped foreign tourists in southeast Turkey, including 19 seized in eight separate incidents on July 5, 1993. In each case, the foreign tourists were well-treated and eventually released unharmed. Since then, kidnappings have been rare until recently when three German climbers were taken hostage in Eastern Turkey. They were released unharmed after Turkish military units pursued the terrorists into Iraq. As Turkey pressures the PKK in Northern Iraq and the US and NATO forces continue the war on terror kidnapping for publicity by Muslim groups is an active threat to those visiting Turkey.

• Hijacking of airplanes. Hijacking is more common in Turkey than in most other countries. Turkey is home to various terrorist and criminal organizations ranging from Islamic groups, left wing radicals to the Albanian Mafia. One recent case in August 2007 a flight that was hijacked in Northern Cyprus was diverted to Antalya in southern Turkey where all passengers were released unharmed, as is the case with the majority of hijackings in Turkey.

• Bombings and Attacks. Over the past few years terrorist bombing and attacks have become a regular occurrence in Turkey. Targets have included buses, banks, restaurants, hotels and foreign embassies in areas such as Istanbul, Izmir, Mersin, Cesme, Antalya, Kusadasi, Marmaris and Ankara. Many of the devices that have been used have been small and the attacks' motive is to dissuade foreign investment, tourism and to publicize the terrorists causes.

When visiting tourist areas always be vigilant and have your procedures prepared for how to react to a terrorist incident.

Terrorist And Bombing Incidents Include:

• 21 August 2008, a car bomb exploded in a residential area of Izmir, injuring 11 military and police personnel.

• 7 August 2008, 3 people were injured in a mortar attack on a military barracks in Uskudar, Istanbul.

• 27 July 2008, 17 people were killed and many wounded in two explosions in the Gungoren shopping district of Istanbul.

• 9 July 2008, three police officers and three gunmen were killed in an attack on the US consulate in Istanbul.

• 3 January 2008, six people are killed and more than 60 wounded in a car bomb attack on a military bus in the south-eastern city of Diyarbakir.

• 2 October 2007, two explosions in Izmir killed one person and injured five others and a further explosive device did not detonate.

• 11 September 2007, Police defused a large vehicle bomb in the Kurtulus district in Ankara.

• 11 July 2007, an explosion occurred outside the District Governor's office in the Bahçelievler district of Istanbul injuring two.

• 10 June 2007, an explosion occurred in a shopping district in the Bakirkoy district of Istanbul injuring 14 people.

• 22 May 2007, six people are killed and more than 90 injured in a suicide bombing at the entrance to a Shopping Centre in Ankara.

• 5 November 2006, three soldiers are killed, and 14 others wounded when a roadside mine exploded beside a military convoy in south-eastern Turkey.

• 2 October 2006, fifteen people are injured in a blast at a cafe in Izmir, Turkey's third largest city.

- 12 September 2006, eleven people are killed, eight of them children, in a bomb blast in a park in Diyarbakir, a city in the country's south-east.

- 28 August 2006, three people are killed and at least 20 hurt in an explosion in the resort of Antalya. Later, 21 others are injured in three explosions in the southern resort of Marmaris. Another six people are injured in an explosion near the local government's office in the Istanbul district of Bagcilar.

- 4 August 2006, thirteen people are injured in two bomb attacks in southern Turkey. The first bomb explodes near a bank in the city of Adana. The second blast occurs minutes later at a nearby construction site.

- 25 June 2006, four people are killed and 25 injured in an explosion near a restaurant in the resort of Antalya. Initial investigations suggest a gas canister exploded, but it is not known if this was an accident.

- 15 June 2006, an explosion near a bus station in central Istanbul injures three people. Officials say an explosive device was hidden in a rubbish bin in the busy Eminonu district.

- 3 June 2006, fourteen people are injured in an explosion outside a shopping centre in the port city of Mersin. The blast is said to have been caused by a remote-controlled bomb.

- 16 April 2006, thirty-one people are hurt in an explosion in the Bakirkoy district of Istanbul. The blast appears to have been caused by a bomb left in a trash can near a shop.

- 5 April 2006, two people are injured in an explosion at the local offices of the ruling Justice and Development Party (AKP) in Istanbul.

- 31 March 2006, one person dies, and 13 others are injured when a bomb explodes inside a rubbish bin near a bus stop in the Kocamustafapasa district of Istanbul.

- 15 March 2006, two people are injured in an explosion outside an HSBC bank in the southern city of Diyarbakir.

• 13 February 2006, eleven people are hurt in an explosion in front of a supermarket in the Bahcelievler suburb of Istanbul. A Kurdish terrorist group claims responsibility.

Conclusions

• Proper plans need to be put into place to deal with all emergencies while at sea and shore side.

• Personal security needs to be taken seriously by all personnel.

• Personnel should have good means of communications with them at all times and know the contact numbers, separate from their cell phones, for the Motor Yacht and other crew members.

• Shore side crew should regularly check in with the Motor Yacht.

• Emergency rendezvous points and routes need to be arranged as well as emergency methods of transport to the emergency rendezvous points.

• Medical emergencies need to be planned for. Remember, medical facilities may not be up to the standard encountered in the US or EU.

Emergency Service Numbers For Turkey

• Fire: 110
• Medical Emergency: 112 or 144
• Police: 155
• Gendarme: 156
• Coast Security: 158

Emergency Service Numbers For Greece

• Fire: 199 or 112
• Medical Emergency: 166 or 122

- Police: 100 or 112
- Coast Security: 108

List of relevant Embassies and Consulates in Greece and Turkey attached.

CORPORATE THREAT ASSESSMENT IN DOMINICAN REPUBLIC

This assessment was compiled on an investment project for a location that was being developed into a luxury marina and resort in the Dominican Republic. To put it simply the whole project stank from our initial meetings on the island to the time we left.

The clients had done no due diligence and did not like the fact we told them that they were going to have major problems in the future unless they cleaned house. Of course, these clients knew best and within 8-months the whole project had crashed due to disputes over land ownership, things that should have been identified in the initial due diligence that was never done.

Corporate Threat Assessment

11 October 2006   File Number: ####

This assessment will cover potential threats to the physical security of #### staff/clients and additional threats to the overall #### project as seen at this time. If the project progresses, threat assessments will need to be regularly compiled.

Orlando Wilson

Risks Inc.

Overall Considerations

Due Diligence

We were led to believe no due diligence had been compiled on anyone involved in the project. This needs to be done on all investors, buyers and local assets.

Intellectual Property Security

We did not see or hear anything to suggest that there has been any consideration for the protection of the project's intellectual property. We expect information about the project that has been passed to local assets is now common knowledge to those with potential hostile interests in the project.

Communications

It is common knowledge in DR (Dominican Republic) that all phone, fax, e-communications are monitored, and this information can be bought by those with the right contacts. If the project's local counsel has not informed you of this from the start of the project, we would doubt their loyalty.

For serious international communication, e-mail encryption is a must and the project's computer server must be housed in a secure location. There are various methods and equipment available to assist with secure phone and fax communications. For communications between the project's staff, we suggest the use of radios; there were areas where cell phone coverage was not good. In time, base stations should be located at the #### site and the chosen accommodation location. These would need to be monitored while personnel are on the ground.

First Aid & Medical Considerations

We did not see that any consideration had been given to what to do in the case of a medical emergency. Medical facilities in DR can be basic; an in-depth assessment needs to be done on what medical facilities are in the area of the #### site and accommodation location.

The #### site should have first aid trained personnel and a comprehensive first aid kit on location whenever there are visitors/staff present. The state of the #### site at this time could make a casualty evacuation difficult. Visitors and staff travelling the #### site should always have a first aid kit in their vehicles.

There are cases of foreigners contracting malaria and dengue fever from mosquitoes. The relevant precautions need to be taken to prevent infection. Medical insurance will need to be arranged for staff and details of locally accepted policies compiled for visitors. A full medical assessment needs to be completed, if you are dealing with VIPs; the individuals and their insurance companies will expect you to have done this.

General Physical Security

Airport Pick-Up

All pickups from the airport should be kept low profile for staff and clients. The project needs to acquire its own vehicles and trusted drivers for this service. It would make sense not to use the #### name on signs when collecting staff and clients; basic lettered signs should be used and changed on a regular basis. This prevents signs being copied and your staff and clients being taken away and robbed or kidnapped, etc.

We would suggest you speak to airport personnel and have the project drivers meet staff and clients directly at the exit from the airport to save them being harassed by taxi drivers, etc. For VIP clients, a more discreet procedure for entering and exiting the airport will need to be devised. We expect the airport staff would be happy to assist with implementing this for a fee.

Primary and secondary routes need to be selected from the airport to the accommodation. We saw the routes are limited but need to be varied as much as possible. For client pickups, we could suggest a Spanish speaking assistant to be with the driver to help with any problems that may occur on the route. The vehicle should have good communications to keep those at the accommodation location informed of pick up, leaving the airport, any problems etc. A second vehicle needs to be at hand to recover the clients in the case of a break down or accident. For VIP clients, a security person or team should be available in a separate vehicle.

Accommodation Security

The hotel #### appeared to be a well-run hotel in a security-gated complex that should keep out most petty-criminals. One area that had limited security was the beach area; walking into the hotel from there would be easy. The hotel staff were polite and well-mannered, but we saw no security personnel and no firearms.

If the hotel is to be regularly used, staff and clients need to be located in close proximity on the second or third floor and armed plain clothed security personnel should be manning the hallway 24/7. This would be minimal cover and would be expected by VIP clients.

In the future, if the project gets going, and sorts out its own accommodation, full security procedures will need to be implemented. Security should be a major consideration in site selection.

Places Of Entertainment

Reputable and hygienic places of entertainment for staff and clients need to be taken into consideration. An assessment of restaurants and clubs needs to be compiled; not only security needs to be taken into account but also the hygiene of the venue.

While at dinner with the project's local attorney, a large rat was seen walking around the roof of the restaurant. Such a thing could prove to be extremely embarrassing if entertaining clients and can also lead to illness etc.

Recreational transportation for staff and client's needs to be arranged. A list of reputable taxi/car companies should be compiled. For VIP clients, suitable cars, drivers, and security should be available.

Route From Hotel #### To #### Site

It is our understanding that there is one road to the #### site from the accommodation location, which takes about an hour to drive. This road will need to be driven, and a threat assessment compiled.

Helicopters are the best option for moving staff and clients between locations, but arrangements need to be made in case of bad weather or if mechanical problems occur with the helicopter. Due to the state of DR roads, a 4X4 vehicles are suggested.

The #### Site

The #### site has no effective security; we expect the two guards we saw are only present or awake when there are visitors. They were not alert or well-presented and in no way install confidence in their ability.

The #### site has no perimeter fence that can keep out intruders and we expect the site perimeter has never been patrolled or checked. From the small section we drove past on the road to ####, we saw several areas that look as if they were being used to gain access to the site. The site needs a perimeter fence that can keep out trespassers. All entry points need to be blocked off or manned by competent personnel.

Just driving on the roads of the main site we saw tracks that seem to be used, as well as evidence of horse hoof prints. People have free access to this site. Due to the heavy bush and foliage, it would be easy for people to be on the site without being spotted. At the location of the show houses, there were signs that people had been in them recently.

There is also free access to the site from the sea and harbor area. The entrance to the project's part of the harbor area needs to be buoyed off and a small boat made available for security patrols. This boat could also be used for showing clients the waterways.

Due to the complete lack of any perimeter security and dense foliage on the site, it is easy for petty criminals to commit express robberies on the project's staff working at the site or clients viewing the site. More serious crimes would be just as easy to commit.

We would strongly suggest that all staff and client visits to the site are proceeded by advance security and until there is decent perimeter security all senior management, clients, and VIPs, at least, are accompanied by professional armed security personnel while viewing the site.

Reliable vehicles need to be in place at the site for viewing clients and security patrols. ATVs could make a better option for security patrols.

The Security Team

It is quite obvious at this point in time security has in no way been considered in this project. Due to the situation in DR and the high profile of this project all senior staff members and clients should be accompanied by armed security when not in secure areas.

We would suggest the security team to be a combination of expats and local personnel. The minimum number of operational expats we would recommend would be 2 for the first stages of the project and in time expanding this to a team of 4. The expats would be responsible for executive protection, coordination of locals and special tasks.

A well-connected and controllable Dominican security company needs to be employed for the provision of executive protection personnel and regular security personnel. The Dominican personnel would need to be well trained and equipped. The management of the company would need to be well-connected in Santo Domingo to ensure things run smoothly with local police and military agencies. At this point we would estimate approximately 8 to 12 local security and executive protection personnel are required.

The operational procedures and orders for the security team would need a lot of in-depth planning. Issues that would need to be considered would include the provision of firearms permits, etc., for expats.

Other Threats

The main threats we see to the #### projects are what is going on behind the scenes at local and national level. This is a high-profile project and to our knowledge has had problems in the past. DR has a reputation for corruption at all levels, especially where large projects are concerned. We speak from experience!

Money Laundering

We were surprised to hear that apparently no precautions have been considered to prevent #### property being bought for money laundering purposes. This could be a major threat to the whole project. One sale paid for with money from an illicit source could lead to property seizures and problems with law enforcement agencies in DR and U.S. We expect the DR side of things could be put right but it would be costly. If you have competition in this project, this is one angle that could be used against you.

Local Assets

We met with the project's local attorney, "Jesus," and from the start our impression was not favorable. He stated he had never dealt with a contract of this size before and did not have an office in Santo Domingo; he had had a practice in Santo Domingo, but it failed. To be taken seriously in DR, he would need a Santo Domingo office as this is where the politics goes on and where deals are done. With a project with the potential size of ####, you will need seriously connected local attorneys and counsel to prevent problems and ensure things run smoothly.

It appears that "Jesus" has been acting as the project manager unsupervised. We strongly doubt that in the period this project has been dormant that he has been doing nothing but waiting for you to get funding, without looking for other ways to line his pockets.

When asked about the security for the #### site, he stated there were good security personnel in place and that no one had access to the site. We know for a fact he was talking complete and utter rubbish. When asked about security guards for the site, he stated they were looking to use a Bulgarian-run local security company. At one point, he also stated that 2 years ago, one company had bought land near the #### site on which to set up a factory to produce furniture for the project. When asked why this company thought it was going to get the contract, he was not able to answer the question. We expect he sold them the land and guaranteed them the contract. Problems can occur if contracts have been guaranteed to vendors and they are not granted.

When the subject of the peninsula across from the #### site was raised "Jesus" stated he had heard that there had recently been Russians asking about the sale of the land, he stated he did not know who they were. Later in the meeting he stated the Russians had bought property in DR 3 years ago.

"Jesus" stated that he is hiring new attorneys for the #### project, all of whom- from what we heard- are young and female, pretty but with little legal experience. It was also interesting to hear one was a native Russian. He also stated one of his attorneys and himself had recently been approached by "####". As things progress you can expect these approaches to happen a lot more frequently and you must monitor local staff.

One potential problem that needs to be assessed is the town of ####. If the project takes off, the property prices in the area will increase greatly and, from what we saw, the majority of the people in this town are not the wealthiest. We would expect this to lead to property owners evicting local renters, etc. This could lead to political, media and civil problems, if not taken into consideration beforehand.

We would strongly suggest interviewing all local assets that have been connected with the project to determine if they have been working in your interests and not leaking information or contract details. "Jesus" needs to be aggressively interviewed about his official and unofficial dealings concerned with this project.

Due diligence needs to be completed on all local assets. Special attention needs to be paid to the financial dealings of local attorneys to ensure none of their previous business dealings or property deals have been illicit or have involved laundered money.

Everyone involved in any previous problems where money for concessions has been given or granted needs to be investigated. Special attention would need to be paid to these people's personal financial transactions.

Conclusions

The potential threats to the #### project that we see are varied and numerous. The overall threat level of this project is high.

The general threat to the physical security of staff and clients is medium and should be at the normal level for those visiting the Dominican Republic. The threat to senior management will greatly increase as the project develops and political or corruption related problems occur.

The threat from corruption is extremely high at all levels. This should be constantly monitored and expected. Without strong Dominican attorneys and counsel, the threat from corruption is greatly increased.

Estimated Budget

A rough estimate for a security budget for the first 12 months of this project is $##0,000, 00.

Orlando Wilson

11 October 2006

THE CLOSE PROTECTION ORDERS PROCEDURE

After a TA has been compiled and you have agreed to take on the client, orders need to be drawn up for the operation. The term 'orders' is used to describe the planning, preparation and operational procedures for the operation. There should be an overall set of orders for the whole operation and, if necessary, sub-orders should be drawn up to cover such things as a business trip or attending a function.

You need to plan for every eventuality, be it bad weather or a terrorist attack. You are more likely to be rained on than shot at. Everyone on the security team needs to know what he or she is doing and when he or she are meant to do it. You might have the best driver in the world on your team but if he thinks he has to pick up the client at 15:00 hrs instead of knowing he should pick up the client at 14:00 hrs he is useless and could embarrass you and lose you a client. There is no room for mistakes as mistakes are just human error.

When the orders for the operation have been compiled, you need to brief the whole security team on the operation and go into detail on what their individual responsibilities are. The orders for the operation need to be kept secure and confidential. The security team should not discuss any of the timings and procedures with anyone outside of the security team.

When a regular team has been working together for a while they will get to know their procedures by heart. This is a good thing but can also lead to complacency. Orders need to be regularly updated, and procedures practiced.

The following pages outline an example set of orders for an operation. This is a sequence for a set of quick orders; these may be used when you do not have time for a full orders sequence. You will not always need to include every subject in your own order. This orders sequence is based on the British Army format and is adapted for close protection operations.

Close Protection Orders

Overall Sequence

1. Ground

2. Situation:

a. Program

b. The client

c. The threat

d. The enemy

e. Friendly forces

f. Responsibilities

3. Mission

4. Execution

5. Service Support

6. Command and Signals

Quick Orders Sequence

1. Threat

2. Ground

a. Local areas

b. Principal residence location

c. Safe houses

d. Grounds

e. Office locations

f. Routes

g. Places regularly frequented

3. Client's Program

4. Timings

5. Manpower and responsibilities

6. Liaison

7. The client:

a. Likes and dislikes

b. Medical

c. Habits

d. Marital status

e. Family

f. Hobbies

g. Background

8. Logistics

a. Client's Vehicle

b. Team transport

c. Feeding

d. Dress

f. Accommodation

g. Weapons and ammunition

9. Weather

10. Enemies and their M/O

a. Shooting

b. Bombing

c. Kidnap

d. Embarrass

e. Day/night

f. Most likely time of attack

11. Assessment of tasks

12. Conclusions

Example Of Close Protection Orders

Operation Intro

Operation Starts at 0700 on 23/08/99. Duration of operation 4 weeks.

Threat: Medium Level. Due to client's position in a pharmaceutical company there is a threat of physical assault and public disturbances by animal rights protesters.

Ground:

a. Local areas: London, Postal areas SW1, W1, NW3, EC1X.

b. Principals residence location: 12 St Pauls Rd, London, NW3 6TA. Grid 127649

c. Safe houses:

1. 17 Morley Rd, Highgate, London N8 3RE. Grid 687905. Home of Mr P Thomas (company secretary) Tel: 0171 327 2456.

2. 23 Old Hill, Kew, London, SW12 1OP. Home of Ms T Smith (Director) Tel: 0171 457 3987

Contact safe houses at least 30 minutes before Advance security arrives. Take full counter- surveillance procedure on way to safe houses.

d. Grounds: All houses have gardens front and rear.

e. Office locations: An 8-story modern office block at 44 Cheapside, London, EC1X Grid 457890. Client's office on 8th floor.

f. Routes: The client travels regularly in the SW1, W1, NW3, EC1X Postal code areas of London. Client has his own chauffeur who knows London well. Team are advised to stick to main road. There are regular problems in these areas with traffic jams and road works.

g. Places regularly frequented:

1. Eton Gents Club, Balford Sq., London, W1. Tel 0171 435 2567.

2. Madam Rubies, Hostess club, 12 Shapers St, London, SW1. Tel 0171 456 7890

3. St. George's, Golf Club, Watford, HW5 T5. Tel 0128 678 5987.

Client's Program: The client works from 0900 to approx. 1700, Monday to Friday at his office and then usually goes to one of his favorite clubs to socialize until around 1900. He then goes home. At weekends, the client likes to spend time at home or at the golf club, where he spends most of his time in the clubroom.

Timings: Operation Starts at 0700 on 23/08/99, you will be on call until the end of the operation

THREAT ASSESSMENTS

Manpower and responsibilities: Team of 5 CPOs, Team leader and personnel BG is Tom. Initially Mike and Pete will take turns at being No 2 BG and advance security and additional tasks. Sid and Harry will be responsible for the security of the residence, (12 hour on 12 hour off shifts)

Liaison: Tom is the liaison with the client; any problems should be directed through him. Local Police Liaison is PC Plod of Hampstead police Tel: 0171 998 7676. Emergency Tel: 999

The client: Mr Williby Simpson-Gomm

a. Likes and dislikes: The client is 57 yr. old and is very "Old School". Dislikes bad manners and being called by his first

name by people who are not his close friends. Always address as Sir or Mr Simpson-Gomm. The client likes flirting with

young ladies. Maximum discretion must be shown at all times.

b. Medical: Minor heart condition. GP is Mr Kapoor, 56 Heath Drive, Hampstead, London, NW4 WS4. Emergency Tel: 08990 87659. Hospitals: See List.

c. Habits: Cigar Smoker, drinks approx. 8 shots of spirits a day.

d. Marital status: Married. Wife's name Mrs Sara Simpson-Gomm (54 years old). To be addressed as Madam or Mrs Simpson-Gomm. She knows of his liking for younger ladies and is a heavy drinker. A very temperamental lady. If any problems are encountered with her, report them to Tom.

e. Family: Two Grown up children. Rupert, 28. Lives in New York. Hanna, 25 currently traveling around the world.

f. Hobbies: The client is a workaholic, when not working relaxes reading or the odd game of golf.

g. Background: The client has been in the pharmaceutical business since 1971. He formed WSG-Industries in 1985. He is the companies CEO and is outspoken in his view that it is OK to test new medicines etc. on animals

Logistics:

a. Clients Vehicle: Black Bentley, VRN WSG-1.

b. Team Transport: 2 BGs will travel with the client. Advance security as a motorbike available. Spare car available at residence.

c. Feeding: Meals taken at residence or at client's location.

d. Dress: BGs, Business suit during the week as per client requirement during the weekend. Advance Security, smart casual dress. Residential, smart casual

f. Accommodation: BG-AS at client's residence. Residential, own arraignments.

g. Weapons and ammunition: under UK law no weapons are to be carried of any description.

Weather: UK summer. Hot and humid with rain showers.

Enemy and their M/O: Various animals right's protesters. Usually very educated and ruthless in the execution of their attacks. Usual form of attack is the use of small firebombs and letter bombs. Also be aware of the threat of embarrassment that public disturbances might cause.

Notes:

EXAMPLE OF INDUSTRIAL SECURITY SITE ORDERS

The following images are of a set of assignment orders (Assignment Instructions) for a sensitive manned security contract in the UK. This location and the security company that had the contract have long since shut down, so its OK for me to share the documents.

From what is listed below you will be able to see what should be included in professional site orders. Each set of site orders need to be adapted specifically to the locations, the needs of the client and the threats identified in the threat assessment. Site orders for a residence would of course be significantly different from those below due to the different nature of the threats, duties involved and locations.

ORLANDO "ANDY" WILSON

ASSIGNMENT INSTRUCTIONS

Site Copy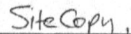

These assignment instructions have been prepared to detail those aspects of the customer's contract that are specific to the client, and may be in addition to, or at variance with, the standard Quality System Procedures. Therefore, this document must be read in conjunction with any related company procedures.

ASSIGNMENT NAME AND ADDRESS

ASSIGNMENT TELEPHONE NUMBER

ASSIGNMENT FAX NUMBER

PERSONS RESPONSIBLE FOR SECURITY

Mr Kevin

OUT OF HOURS CONTACTS

THE FIRST POINT OF CONTACT FOR ANY PROBLEM IS MR KEVIN .... OR THE DUTY ENGINEER. THEIR CONTACT NUMBERS CAN BE FOUND IN THE ASSIGNMENT LOG.

THIS INFORMATION IS STRICTLY CONFIDENTIAL AND MUST NOT BE DIVULGED TO ANYONE

CONTACT NUMBERS

DUTY CONTROLLER (17.30 to 09.30)

Head Office :
Telephone :
Fax :
E-Mail :

DIRECTOR OF OPERATIONS -

MANAGING DIRECTOR -

DIRECTOR -

CHECK CALLS TO BE MADE **HOURLY** ON NIGHT SHIFT, AT WEEKENDS AND ON BANK HOLIDAYS

List of attachments:

OPERATIONS LOG
ASSIGNMENT LOG
CONTRACTORS BOOK
VISITORS BOOK

.... operate a Quality Management System to the requirements of BS EN ISO9002. Customers are requested to assist this process by approving and returning a copy of these instructions. Instructions not returned within 10 days of issue will be deemed acceptable.

Approved: ....
(On behalf of the Client)
Date: 3/6/97

Distribution:
2 Copies to client (less attachments) - signed copy to be returned.
1 Copy to site log - 1 Copy to Control Room (less attachments)
1 Copy to Contract file (less attachments)

Page 1 of 2
Issue: 2
Review date: **APRIL 1998**

THREAT ASSESSMENTS

ASSIGNMENT INSTRUCTIONS

Hours of Work

Monday to Thursday	17.30 - 09.00 hours
Friday	17.30 - 07.00 hours
Saturday	07.00 - 19.00 hours
	19.00 - 07.00 hours
Sunday	07.00 - 19.00 hours
	19.00 - 09.00 hours } Including Bank Holidays

Manning Levels

1 Security Officer

PATROLLING

~~Random EXTERNAL patrol duties (frequency not specified)~~ N.

- Check computer rooms
- Check that windows are closed
- Check internal fire doors are closed
- Check lights are switched off
- Note and report obstructions in fire escapes routes
- Check that break glasses and fire appliances are operable
- Check for leaks - especially in toilets and vending areas
- Check all PAC security doors are functioning correctly
- Check fire phones, fire equipment, and panic buttons are operational
- Check kitchens

N.B. NO EXTERNAL PATROLS ARE TO BE MADE

UNDER NO CIRCUMSTANCES IS THE SECURITY OFFICER TO LEAVE THE BUILDING TO INVESTIGATE AN INCIDENT (OR FOR ANY OTHER REASON) IF HELP IS REQUIRED HE IS TO CALL ASSISTANCE FROM EITHER CONTROL OR THE EMERGENCY SERVICES

RECEPTION DUTIES

- Receive telephone calls and deal with client requests
- Liaise with ▓▓▓▓▓▓▓▓▓▓▓▓▓ personnel
- Check visitors and contractors in and out of the premises
- Check in-coming 'by hand' deliveries
- Issue keys to authorised personnel

	MANNED SECURITY GUARDING	ISSUE: 1 PAGE 1 of 6
Prepared by:		Approved by:

PURPOSE

This procedure details the controls to be exercised in respect of Manned Guarding Assignments.

CONTENTS

General.
Assignment Report.
Assignment Instructions.
Incident reports.
Patrols.
Standing orders.

QUALITY RECORDS

Assignment Report.
Incident report.
Operations Book.
Supervisors Shift Report.
Assignment Instructions

MANNED SECURITY GUARDING	ISSUE: 1
	PAGE 2 of 6

GENERAL

Each manned security site shall be issued with an Site Log Book which shall contain the following:
- **Assignment Reports**;
- Assignment Instructions;
- Blank **Incident Reports**.

Term 'Controller' used in this procedure shall be read as:
<u>Nights</u>
Control Room
<u>Days</u>
Control Room - for Booking-on/off duty and Check Calls.
Director of Operations or Duty Manager - For occurrences, incidents or other emergencies (except which reports to Control Room).

Additionally, the management team may be contacted, in the event of emergencies, 24 hours per day.

Each site shall hold a **Operations Book** which shall be used to record all occurrences that are not anticipated or part of a routine. Details of the occurrence and the resulting action taken shall be summarised, as follows:
- Date;
- Entry - (Next sequential No, Details of occurrence and actions taken);
- Signature / Time.

ASSIGNMENT REPORT

At the start of duty the Security Officer shall initiate an **Assignment Report**, to cover the shift. This document could be considered a legal document in the event of a dispute and **must** be used to record all activities undertaken on behalf of the company and the client.

Occurrences and Incidents may be summarised with suitable crossed reference to the **Operations Book** entry and **Incident Report**, where applicable.

It is essential that activities and duties are entered as they occur, on no account must the entries be left and entered at the end of a shift.

If visiting supervision find this has happened, a Non-conformance and Corrective Action Report shall be issued and disciplinary action taken.

Assignment Reports shall be sent to Head Office on a monthly basis.

Note: Sites that are 'supervised' may have a specific **Supervisors Shift Report** developed to replace the **Assignment Report**. As the format and content of these will vary, to suit the needs of the site, they shall be developed as an attachment to the associated set of **Assignment Instructions**.

MANNED SECURITY GUARDING	ISSUE: 1
	PAGE 3 of 6

ASSIGNMENT INSTRUCTIONS

The Security Officer shall make him/herself aware of the **Assignment Instructions** and record this on the **Assignment Report**. Instructions that cannot be located or require clarification shall be reported to the Quality Representative.

In the event of the client giving instructions to vary any requirement, name or contact in the **Assignment Instructions**, details shall be recorded on the **Assignment Report**.

INCIDENT REPORTS

An incident is a serious occurrence that is not part of the routine (e.g. fire, break-in, assault or flooding). All incidents are to be recorded using the **Incident Report**, it is essential that the incident is fully documented. The report shall be completed as soon as practical after the incident and shall detail the times and sequence of events.

The Security Officer shall take the most appropriate course of action in respect of each incident, including notification to the controller and the emergency services, where applicable.

The Security Officer shall, at all times, avoid placing him/herself at risk.

Depending on the nature of an 'Incident', the report may become the basis of a claim by the company or the client.

Remember if in doubt raise an **Incident Report**.

Incident Reports shall be submitted to Head Office at the earliest opportunity. Copies may be given to the client's representative, where appropriate. The original shall be retained in the Site Log Book for a minimum of 3 months and then may be destroyed.

Note: Certain clients require **Incident Reports** to be presented in a different format to the company standard, in such cases these will be developed as attachments to the associated assignment instructions.

PATROLS

Patrols shall be carried out to the times and frequency detailed in the **Assignment Instructions**, the times and duration being recorded on the **Assignment Report**.

MANNED SECURITY GUARDING	ISSUE: 1
	PAGE 4 of 6

STANDING ORDERS

The following standing orders form the principal procedures and duties of all Security Officers and unless varied to meet the requirements of particular assignments, are to be adhered to at all times.

Objectives:
- To protect the property of the client against fire, theft, damage and intruders.
- To ensure that no unauthorised persons or vehicles enter the clients premises and that those who are authorised are courteously dealt with.
- To ensure that no personnel including contractors, or any vehicle leaves the clients premises in an irregular manner.
- To render any assistance to the client or his personnel in any emergency.
- To record fully any unusual occurrence or incident as required.
- If breaches of industrial discipline, including infringement of the Health and Safety at Work Act are observed, action is to be confined to immediately reporting the matter to the clients representative and recording as above. Only if there is immediate risk and danger should the Security Officer intervene.
- Personal searches are not to be carried out without prior agreement in writing.
- Security Officers will be punctual in commencing their tour of duty and be in a fit and proper condition for their duties. They must not leave their assignment without permission or until relieved in the normal way.
- Every effort must be made to notify the controller as early as possible of impending absenteeism so that a relief can be arranged.
- If possible, Security Officers absent through sickness or other reasons shall inform the controller of their intended return at the earliest opportunity.
- Security Officers are to familiarise themselves with all assignment instructions. Variations to such instructions given by control or the client shall be recorded on the **Assignment Report**.
- Security Officers shall abide by any customer site specific rules (e.g. No smoking policy);
- Upon commencement of duty, Security Officers shall confirm the accuracy of records relating to customer property (e.g. Key Registers);
- All instructions to Security Officers are deemed to be confidential and must only be imparted to those with a `need to know'. Any infringement without good reason will be considered a disciplinary offence.
- The Security Officer is in a privileged position within a client's organisation and may in such circumstances have knowledge which is confidential to the client. Such knowledge must be treated as above

MANNED SECURITY GUARDING	ISSUE: 1
	PAGE 5 of 6

Basic functions of a Security Officer:
- To carry out the duties as detailed in the Assignment Instructions.
- To carry out duties as verbally issued by Representatives or clients on our behalf.
- To safeguard the client's employees and property from Fire, Flood, Theft, Trespass, Vandalism and any other risk.
- To prevent accidents by reporting faulty equipment or hazard, in the line of Health & Safety Regulations.
- To record all occurrences, however minor they may seem, in the **Operations Book** and **Assignment Report**.
- To report all incidents to the controller with details being recorded via an **Incident Report**.
- To work in a manner that is safe both to themselves and other persons as required under Health and Safety Legislation.
- Ensure that any probationer at the assignment is familiar with standing orders and the assignment procedures.

Site Log Book :
- Your **Assignment Report** must be used to record all that happens whilst you are on duty, this is to include time on/off duty, receipt of clients keys, times check calls are made, out and in patrol times, plus all occurrences that effect security.
  All occurrences must be recorded in the **Assignment Report** and **Operations Book**. A serious occurrence shall be recorded in detail on an **Incident Report** with an entry of reference made on the **Assignment Report**.
- Entries must be in Blue or Black ink and be written clearly and precisely in plain English.

Book On/Off Procedures:
- Security Officers, on unsupervised sites, arriving for duty must 'Book-on' with the controller personally.
- Always ensure you 'Book-on' at the correct time, clearly stating your name. (Any Officers booking on after the official start time will be booked on at time of call and will only receive payment from that time).
- Security Officers who are not relieved by an oncoming guard, within 15 minutes of their shift ending, must notify control. The Officer shall remain on site until relieved, and notify control of the time of relief.

Check Calls:
- Security Officers, on unsupervised sites, are required in accordance with Health & Safety policies to make Check Calls. These are to give an assurance that both you and the premises you are guarding are safe.
- Check Calls must be made at the prescribed time you are allocated, and at the correct frequency allotted to your assignment.
- On making a Check Call, you must state your name clearly, also mentioning anything untoward that may have occurred since your last call.
- Failure to make a Check Call will result in a call from the controller after a waiting period and a possible visit by a duty manager if no response is gained or if the controller feels that the respondent is not Bona Fide. The Police may also be informed and requested to attend site.

THREAT ASSESSMENTS

MANNED SECURITY GUARDING	ISSUE: 1
	PAGE 6 of 6

Radio use:
- Assignments that have two-way radios must have them switched on at all times.
- Radios are only to be used for routine or emergency calls and not for conversation purposes between guards.
- All calls over radio must commence with your call sign directed to the call sign you require.

Uniform Dress:
- Security Officers when on duty must be in the company uniform, or that specified by the client.
- Black plain shoes or boots must be worn.
- Ties must always be worn.
- Epaulettes must always be worn on shirts or NATO jumpers.
- Full uniform must be worn at all times whilst on duty, any guards found to be not wearing uniform will be subject to disciplinary procedures.
- Uniforms must remain in a clean and tidy state, a clean and pressed shirt shall be worn for each shift, any defective item must be reported to Head Office for replacement.
- I.D. Cards are part of company uniform and must be worn or carried at all times whilst on duty.
- No weapons 'real' or 'imitation' will be carried on duty. Not even for self defence.
- Security Officers must be freshly shaved before commencing duty.

Disciplinary matters:
Listed below are some examples which, if not adhered to, will lead to disciplinary action and possible dismissal from the company.
- Failure to be dressed in proper uniform.
- Poor time keeping.
- Poor standard of work.
- Unauthorised, unreasonable and/or repeated absences (this can include certified sickness).
- Unauthorised presence at work.
- Disruptive behaviour.
- Smoking in any other than authorised areas.
- Abusive or insulting language.
- Fighting with, or injury to a fellow member of the company.
- Drinking of alcohol on duty or just prior to commencement of duty.
- Taking of non-prescribed drugs on duty or prior to duty.
- Leaving an assignment without proper relief or permission from the controller.
- Sleeping on duty.
- Damage, theft or neglect of company or client's property.
- Breach of Health & Safety or Hygiene Policies.
- Use of client's telephones for personal use.
- Allowing access to client's premises of unauthorised persons.
- Use of client's equipment without prior permission.
- Breach of either client or company confidentiality.

ORLANDO "ANDY" WILSON

Orlando has worked internationally at all levels of the specialist security and investigation industry for over 35 years. Over the years, he has become accustomed to the types of complications that can occur, when dealing with international law enforcement agencies and the problem of dealing with kidnapping, organized crime and Mafia groups.

His experience in the international security business began in 1988 when he enlisted in the British army at 17 years of age and volunteered for a 22-month frontline, operational tour in Northern Ireland in an Infantry unit, 4 Platoon, 1 WFR. He then joined his unit's Reconnaissance Platoon, with which he undertook intensive training in small-unit warfare.

Since leaving the British army in 1993, his time spent working in Eastern Europe in the 1990s gave him firsthand experience of the operational procedures of organized criminals and Mafia groups from the former Soviet Union. In addition, he had the opportunity to oversee criminal cases that have been the first of their kind in their respective country. His operations in Mexico training tactical police teams put him in a unique position to understand the war on Narco-Terrorism.

His continuous and ongoing projects focusing on kidnap and ransom prevention in South America, the Caribbean and West Africa have given him the knowledge to formulate practical programs to counter the kidnapping threat.

Orlando is a published author, writer, photographer and has been interviewed by numerous international TV and media outlets on topics ranging from kidnapping, organized crime to maritime piracy. He had his first article published in 1997 in an association magazine and his first book in 2012. He has been interviewed by media outlets ranging from the Professional Mariner Magazine, Newsweek Serbia, Newsweek en Espanol, GrupoMilenio, MundoFox, The New York Times, the BBC, Soldier of Fortune Magazine and others.

Orlando's diverse and continuous operational experience enables him to provide no-nonsense professional services and training programs. His operational investigation and close protection procedures are cutting edge and the most effective commercially available. He is also a founding member and operations manager of Risks Incorporated.

OTHER BOOKS BY ORLANDO
These Books are Available on Amazon!

Non-Fiction Manuals

- Social Navigation: A Practical Survival Guide for Human Interactions
- Counter Insurgency Operations: A tactical Guide for Law Enforcement
- Intelligence Gathering: Front Line HUMINT Considerations
- Caribbean Security Threats: A threat assessment for the islands of the Caribbean
- Gun Range Management: A Guide for Range Managers, Range Safety Officers & Firearms Instructors
- Investigative Journalist Security: Staying Alive to Tell the Truth
- Threat Assessments for Close Protection & Security Management
- Protecting Your Loved Ones: Security Awareness for Parents & Adults
- Close Protection: Luxury & Hostile Environments
- Close Protection & Firearms
- The Close Protection Business
- Home & Office Security: Protection of Residencies & Businesses
- Travel Security: Personal Travel & Vehicle Security
- Counter Terrorism: Terrorist Attack Response
- Kidnap & Ransom: The Essentials of Kidnapping Prevention
- Shoot First & Shoot Last: The Real-World Guide to Pistol Craft

Crime Fiction

- The Shoot: An Assassin's World
- Vengeance: The Art of Pain
- The Collectors: Death is Easy, Life is Hard
- Reglas Mexicanas: A Life Without Pain, Is Not A Life

Photo Books

- Athens Lockdown 2020 in Pictures
- Wandering in Serbia
- Vigilantes of Imo – Nigerian Vigilante Life in Pictures

www.ingramcontent.com/pod-product-compliance
Lightning Source LLC
Chambersburg PA
CBHW070429180526
45158CB00017B/935